PSALMICS

REV. RICARDO MONTANO

WESTBOW
PRESS®
A DIVISION OF THOMAS NELSON
& ZONDERVAN

WestBow Press books may be ordered through booksellers or by contacting:

WestBow Press
A Division of Thomas Nelson & Zondervan
1663 Liberty Drive
Bloomington, IN 47403
www.westbowpress.com
844-714-3454

All scripture quotations are taken from the King James Version.

ISBN: 978-1-6642-9077-8 (sc)
ISBN: 978-1-6642-9078-5 (hc)
ISBN: 978-1-6642-9076-1 (e)

Library of Congress Control Number: 2023901697

Print information available on the last page.

WestBow Press rev. date: 02/03/2023

INTRODUCTION

The psalms are poetry, but they are also flights for the soul. In their reading, we experience the spiritual magic of the presence of God caressing us and becoming a sensation of incomparable satisfaction, which through human emotions, moves us to the peace and comfort of the kingdom of God. They are a sample of what we feel now and what we will have later. The philosophy of human knowledge is the explanation of consequences after the fact. But God's wisdom is instructions before the facts to avoid consequences. God is wise.

The entire Bible is inspired by God, but the psalms possess a special and dedicated ministration of the Holy Spirit, making them much more intimate with the divinity. And in every letter, word, and expression of these songs emanate the spiritual essence of the heavenly author through the human voices and hands that recorded it in humanity's historical time. In the psalms flows the heart of God.

The book of Psalms has been studied, commented on, and preached in every possible way, with all kinds of theological and doctrinal approaches. Therefore, I do not intend to shed new light or the latest discoveries but only to pour out the joy of the soul produced by these beautiful declarations of love and the ideas God has placed in my mind during reading it. Nor will we address all the psalms but only those on which God leads me to reflect on.

Thank God for His immense mercy. Thank you, readers, for your kindness. Blessings to all.

PSALM 1

Psalm 1 begins where everything should have been but never was: "Blessed is the man that walketh not in the counsel of the ungodly, nor standeth in the way of sinners, nor sitteth in the seat of the scornful." We all, consciously or unconsciously, have been on the wrong side. To follow the advice of the wicked is not to make a mistake in choosing the furnishing of the house or the appropriate brand of car. It is engaging in decisions that negatively affect our personal, spiritual relationships with God. The way of sinners is our past, where we traveled without looking or thinking of God, when our pleasures silenced the call of the Holy Spirit. The chair of the mockers is the position of the legalists and religious who stand as judges, relegating to a second place the unique and exclusive authority of God to make judgments. This verse is only fulfilled when it is attributed to Jesus of Nazareth, the Son of God.

The second verse is pure love: "But his delight is in the law of the Lord; and in his law doth he meditates day and night." Anything that becomes our delight will occupy most of our time and thoughts. Nowadays, it has become fashionable to reduce services, shorten sermons, and end services in the church as quickly as possible. By doing this, we are belittling God and demonstrating indifference to Him. Imagine someone who does not want to spend time listening or talking to his partner, always presenting an excuse to leave quickly. Obviously, he does not love her. When we do not eagerly seek biblical knowledge, are unable to stand the Word of God and the presence of God for a long time, and do not wish to preach or listen to a well-grounded doctrinal sermon, even if it takes time, I am deeply sorry to have to say it, but these are signs of a lack of love for God. Delighting in the scriptures and deepening them with perseverance to receive the revelation of divine wisdom is an imperative of the Christian life.

The third verse is a promise of blessing that God bestows on all who choose the path of sacrifice: "And he shall be like a tree planted by the rivers of water, that bringeth forth his fruit in his season; his leaf also shall not wither; But there is a tree that amazes him among all, the good tree that bears good fruit" (Matthew 7:17), which is none other than the tree of the gospel planted next to streams of living water flowing from Jesus and His words. Trees are symbols of growth, strength, and stability. The Word of God is what provides these three factors of spiritual consolidation motivating an optimal growth that includes reaching the height, width, and depth necessary to achieve reach, amplitude, and depth. To grow without increasing is to grow with deficiencies.

The growth of a tree happens in three directions: downward, to acquire stability and firmness (roots); upward, to obtain stature (foliage); and thickness, to have strength (trunk). In the same way, integral spiritual growth must happen. We must first grow down (roots) to have a solid foundation based on biblical knowledge that feeds us of God. Then we must rise in stature to increase the range of vision (foliage). And finally, we must expand the diameter of the trunk to extend our ministry and have the strength to resist the onslaught of the enemy of souls.

In the same way, it must happen in integral spiritual growth. We must first grow downward (have roots) that serve as a solid foundation based on biblical knowledge. Then we must rise in stature (concretize the faith) to increase the range of action and the radius of vision (foliage). Finally, we must strengthen the trunk of our spiritual trees to optimize the effectiveness of the ministry and extend it to the maximum.

The season of fruit will come in God's time. Our mission is to do the work entrusted: "Go ye therefore, and teach all nations, baptizing them in the name of the Father, and of the Son, and of the Holy Ghost" (Matthew 28:19). Then the fruits will be given by God: "And the Lord added to the Church daily such as should be saved" (Acts 2:47). The leafy foliage of the tree of good fruit will never fade or disappear because it is nourished with the power of living water that gives life, and everything that is realized with the energy coming from the divine source of the Holy Spirit will prosper unfailingly. It is not up to us; it is God who does it.

We have no reason to hesitate in fulfilling the purposes that have been entrusted to us. Instead, we have many promises of confirmation and assurance that God will be at the forefront of combat, constantly protecting us: "Have not I commanded thee? Be strong and of a good courage; be not afraid, neither be thou dismayed: for the Lord thy God is with thee whithersoever thou goest" (Joshua 1:9).

Verse 4 points in the opposite direction: "The ungodly are not so: but are like the chaff which the wind drive away." Being a criminal is not the only possible way to be bad. To depart from the goodness of God's Word to walk in the wickedness of the world given to the service of sin is to become one of the wicked. To live turning your back on God without having any divine spirituality controlling the character and personality, to reject Jesus Christ, to despise His teachings, and to disdain the eternal salvation of the soul is to be one of the wicked. Wickedness as a personal attitude is not obligatory. We can reject it by exercising the power and authority given to us by the presence of the Holy Spirit: "But ye shall receive power, after that the Holy Ghost is come upon you" (Acts 1:8).

The bad guys have a universal problem; they are not firm or safe anywhere because they are slaves to the unstable circumstances caused by their behaviors "They are like the chaff which the wind drive away." The chaff is like ashes or dust, which have no weight to hold them in place. Therefore, the wind drags them and disperses them until they disappear. The Bible says in Ephesians 4:14, "that we henceforth be no more children, tossed to and from, and carried about with every wind of doctrine, by the sleight of men, and cunning craftiness, whereby they lie in wait to deceive."

Verse 4 speaks of the temporal consequences faced by the wicked, but verse 5 describes the consequences with eternal meaning: "Therefore the ungodly shall not stand in the judgment, nor sinners in the congregation of the righteous." The basic principle of judgment against the wicked and sinners is the righteousness of God. It is done with righteous judgment, as described in John 5:30: "I can of mine own self do nothing: as I hear, I judge; and my judgment is just; because I seek not mine own will, but the will of the Father which hath sent me." We must understand that to be just is not to be tolerant but to give everyone what he or she deserves. Imagine a lawbreaker brought before a judge and good people who do not punish the crimes of the accused out of pity or sympathy for the offender. That is not justice; it is indolence and irresponsibility. The main foundation of divine justice is fairness. God is no respecter of persons (Romans 2:11). The merits before God are not the positions but the actions. The fundamental objective of the judgment is the separation of the believer from the unbeliever. Because the believers feel uncomfortable among the unbelievers, they do not become contaminated by the wickedness of the unbeliever. On the day of the harvest, the tares will be tied in bunches and thrown into the fire, and the wheat will be gathered and put in the Lord's barn (Matthew 13:30).

The condemnation of the wicked is the result of their decisions contrary to the Word of God. "For if we sin willfully after that we have received the knowledge of the truth, there remaineth no more sacrifice for sins, but a certain fearful looking for of judgment and fiery indignation, which shall devour the adversaries" (Hebrews 10:26–27). The righteous must clearly define their positions of holiness with testimonies of obedience and faith so the wicked and sinners understand that without a change of nature, a change of attitude is impossible.

The final verse separates the destinies: "For the Lord knoweth the way of the righteous: but the way of the ungodly shall perish." The Bible expressly states in Romans 3:10, "As it is written: There is none righteous, no, not one." So, if there is not a single righteous person, to which righteous people does this verse refer? Simple. To those who have been justified by faith in Jesus Christ. We cannot justify ourselves; God justifies us by seeing our ways of faith. Being justified by God does not eliminate the fact that we are sinners by inheritance, but it changes our positions in the face of sin. Previously, we were active sinners, separated and lost, but now we are repentant, forgiven, and justified sinners.

The paths we follow have been straightened before God to lead us to divine grace, where we undeservedly receive reconciliation and relationship with God as well as the salvation of our lives.

"But the way of the ungodly shall perish." The words *trail* and *path* are synonymous, but we can establish a conceptual difference between them. A path is the official route, and a trail is a variant. Going down the trail is not the same as taking the path. And in this lies the difference: The righteous take the official path established by God, and the wicked follow the optional trail they've chosen. The trail avoids the path to shorten distances and reduce time; the roads subdue with self-denial the obstacles to conquer the destinies. The trail is dangerous because they are traveled without intention of transforming them. They are used, not appreciated. The path is safe because it changes conditions by eliminating adversity to create new pathways. The paths, when the grass grows, disappear. The roads, despite the inclement weather, always remain.

PSALM 13

Human beings think they must receive everything needed where they are, without excuses or pretexts. We believe that we have the right to constant and immediate attention. Nothing can be missing or delayed, and if something happens that discourages us, we despair and become depressed to the degree of complaint and reproach. The reality is that the difficulties often outweigh the facilities, and what we think is something safe dissipates in front of our sight and goes down other paths. Even though we are very consecrated, with a life of fervent prayer and total surrender to faith in Christ, prayers may not be answered immediately, or at least in a prudential time, and then all adversity seems to be rampant against us and the circumstances around us. At that moment, the perennial question appears to our lips: "How long wilt thou forget me,

O Lord?" And the answer is: Until we become stronger and learn enough to reduce pride and match needs with God's will.

Often the requests we make seek to satisfy our vanities and not our needs. James 4:3 says, "Ye ask, and receive not, because ye ask amiss, that ye may consume it upon your lust." The root of personal dissatisfaction comes from the misconception of the requests we make. God does not supply for the vagaries of the flesh; He provides for spiritual truths. Our requests must be to strengthening the faith, ministerial growth, blessing of the church, and matters related to the spread of the gospel. As for us, God knows what we really need, and walking the path of faith with Him, we will see His hand providing for us decently.

First the despair, now the anguish. Forever? Of course not. God never forgets the needy; He is forging a better purpose for Himself. When we feel distressed, we are likely to search for feelings to lessen and substitute for the lack of affection and thoughts of prolonged abandonment. We try to imitate alternative moods to supplant the pain. Although we do not realize these mental processes are happening, they manifest themselves as depressive reactions to adversities. The believer must trust God and persevere in the power of the Holy Spirit as an antidote to grief, keeping in mind that everything that happens is God's will, and God's will be the best thing that can happen. We think stress, because we feel it as something interior, arises within us or that we are the cause of it. But it is not so. Stress is an external influence that exerts pressure on one's inner strength. When that external oppression affects internal energy, an emotional imbalance occurs that brings distrust and discomfort to the human form, and to one's spiritual self, doubt and fear. When this happens, we must do the proper spiritual work so as not to live crushed but to reemerge in the freedom with which Jesus delivered us.

The sadness continues with a heartbreaking lament, "How long wilt thou hide thy face from me?" This phrase expresses David's despair. Just as he had previously felt Jehovah had forgotten him, he now felt that he was hiding from Him. But what we take for granted according to feelings is not always according to the facts. The spiritual truth is that God was there, but David could not realize it because his heart was overwhelmed by human problems. David was spiritually blind for the Spirit is not perceived from the flesh. God is omnipresent, which means He is always present in all places at the same time. He has constantly been, is, and will be with us in all circumstances, only in diverse ways. But the gift of discernment of spirits (1 Corinthians 12:10) allows us to find Him during trials.

The feeling of loneliness does not come from the absence of companionship but from the lack of hope. We feel alone when we have exhausted all resources because if there are possibilities, we will not be overwhelmed by feelings of abandonment. It is unshakable faith that fills the gaps of discouragement. The total conviction of God's action, blessing, and provision will not allow spiritual decay to break our convictions. Live by faith, and reality will change.

The second verse shows a different facet of despair, frustration: "How long shall take counsel in my soul, having sorrows in my heart daily? How long shall mine enemy be exalted over me?" The first negative consequence of frustration is considering that everything we have done has been in vain, that we have not obtained any desired results despite the efforts made, so it is not worth continuing to invest time and energies in the project. This comes from not understanding that spiritual processes are progressive, not instantaneous. Victories in God are like growing crops; they are not reaped on the day they are sown. We must spend time taking care of the crops and waiting for their fruit.

David's mistake was that in his despair, anguish, sadness, and frustration, he put his counsel in his soul and did not turn to Jehovah. Solutions cannot be found in consciousness, thoughts, or personal decisions, where problems begin. Individual perceptions should not be used as reference points in conflict resolution. Only in God's Word will we find the right answers to the way out of our problems. Because of his perceptual placement error, David's heart was filled with sadness, one of the main elements of spiritual deterioration, which drained his desire, inspiration, and tenacity. David was in crisis. Sometimes we trust God to do things, rather than doing things while trusting God. From this inversion of the elements of spiritual action come many of the frustrations that sadden us.

The enemies that haunt us have not been exalted by God. *We* give them strength when we are weak. David thought that since God had abandoned him, he had to solve the problems by himself. By making mistakes in his decisions, the enemies took advantage of him. David lost his composure and then broke down into regrets. In general, the problems we face in our relationships with God and with humankind relate to the development in three fundamental areas of the human existential core: God, us, and the world. We are not alone in life, so it is especially important how we interact with the spiritual, social, and personal environments that surround us. The believer's life also includes the doubts, fears, and indecisions common to all mortals. Remember that our Lord Jesus Christ was also a, "man of sorrows" (Isaiah 53:3).

Everything that does not come from God can be opposition and serve as confusion in any aspect or situation. Persecutions are not necessarily death threats but can be ill-intentioned criticism or rejection because of our faith. Ties do not mean that they bind us hands and feet but that they prevent us from preaching. In our day, we must not belittle the enemy because he is very intelligent and subtle. The enemy disguises himself as equality, freedom, and progress and accuses everything that opposes him of discrimination, oppression, and retrograde. The Bible says in 1 Peter 5:8, "Be sober, be vigilant; because your adversary the devil, as a roaring lion, walketh about, seeking whom he may devour." Times have changed, and we are not David. But the enemy remains the same.

David's spiritual reaction, the awakening of hope, begins in the third verse. Humanity's first response to difficulties is born in the innate sinful nature that dominates us internally.

Then, when we understand the mistake we have made and the adversities we created, we realize that we must resort to the spiritual assessment of the situation we face, presenting it to God, the only one who has authority and power to change destinies. That is exactly what David did when he cried out with his soul torn to God, "Consider and hear me, O Lord my God." "Consider and hear me," expresses two aspects of the same clamor: *Consider* is the opposite of, "How long will you hide your face from me?" That single word is crying out, "Keep in mind my existence, which is in danger of ending." The plea, "hear me," means, "Point me to the paths I must follow," and begs of God, "Do not let me let go of Your hand, that without it I will perish." When God looks, it is not just out of curiosity. He has a specific purpose to distinguish and design, to create a reality of blessing and security. God's gaze embraces, includes, and possesses universal reality to mold into the best of divine and human interests. We only need to overcome the inconveniences of life. God's gaze rests upon our efforts.

"Hear me" is the request for another method, along with a new opportunity to be able to carry it out. There is a difference between having a new opportunity and having a second chance. A second chance is the chance to repeat the same thing to improve the initial result. But having a new opportunity is the chance to make everything different so that God's will is fulfilled. In this verse, "Answer me," is synonymous with repentance. David recognizes that he has done wrong and needs to repent to make amends for his attitude. Today we have the precise answer to change the sinful behaviors of our lives: Show we are willing to transform how we are one by the way of faith into the sufficient and eternal sacrifice of Jesus on the cross to receive forgiveness of our sins, and to begin the new opportunity given to us by divine grace and mercy to please God in the future.

Modern society imposes an accelerated and eventful pace of life. Everything changes rapidly, and we never know what is going to happen next. Because of these circumstances, we must constantly ask God for solutions and anxiously cry out, "Answer me, O Jehovah my God!"

Jehovah is unique, the Creator of all that exists, owner of destinies and wills, provider of truths, supplier of needs, and the immense Savior of humankind; that is the incomparable Jehovah. Help only finds answers when they are addressed to Him. David had known the heavenly protective provision before and did not hesitate to resort to it again as he was aware that for Jehovah, it is never too much hassle or takes much insistence. God is always ready to intervene on behalf of His children: "lighten mine eyes, lest I sleep the sleep of death." "Lighten my eyes," is an intercessory prayer for life. In the nearness of death, the brightness and clarity of the gaze vanishes, and new light from God illuminates our eyes and brings life back, brings liberation, and ensures victory. There is a line of connection through the light between God, Jesus, and us: God is Light (1 John 1:5), Jesus is the light of the world (John 8:12), and we are the light in this world (Matthew 5:14). God is light, Jesus brought the light, and we are the reflections of that light. The expression, "lest I sleep the sleep of death," implies that there is another way to sleep. We sleep to death when we conduct ourselves following opinions and criteria based on human knowledge and social customs. But we can sleep to live if we seek the direction of the Holy Spirit and obey God's will.

"Sleeping to death," also means living to die. This is the case of those who deny the spiritual life beyond natural one and indulge in pleasures to take advantage of the time that will run out at any moment. Their life expectancies end in a dark, cold, damp grave. But to sleep to live is living to continue living eternally in the presence of God—if we believe there is a spiritual life beyond this material life and attaining it by obeying by faith in Jesus Christ the commandments of God in the Bible.

"Lest mine enemy say, I have prevailed against him; and those than trouble me rejoice when I am moved." David was Jehovah's anointed king, so if defeated, it would be a defeat for Jehovah as well. That has never happened, and it never will because God is invincible, and our victories depend on the adjudication of that divine invincibility to the adverse circumstances of our lives. It is always important to be recognized as God's representatives so that the victory Jesus achieved on the cross may be glorified in our struggles and strife. The enemy of souls is grotesque, ugly, and unpleasant but appears to be beautiful, appetizing, sensual, and provocative to tempting attract. But the worst enemy we can have and must constantly be aware of is ourselves because of the lust of the flesh (2 Peter 2:18) and the evil desires that are born of the heart (Mark 7:21). If we learn to identify the lies of the evil one using the tools of the Holy Spirit, we can see temptations as warning signs to keep us away from danger.

It is also important to understand that the true believer in Christ has no personal enemies but opponents of the kingdom of God on earth: "for we wrestle not against flesh and blood, but against principalities, against powers, against the rulers of the darkness of this world, against spiritual wickedness in high places" (Ephesians 6:12).

This psalm is an eloquent display of the spiritual trajectory from failure to the joy of victory. It begins with a heartbreaking cry of grief amid the trial, "How long?" Continues to the plunge into the sadness and loneliness of helplessness: "How long shall mine enemy be exalted over me?" And when in a deep depression, he remembers the past blessings and begins to pray, "Consider, answer me, O Jehovah my God." Then comes the joy of having the assurance of the promises begins to flow in the soul, not for their merits, but for the mercy of God: "But I have trusted in thy mercy; my heart shall rejoice in thy salvation." Salvation from danger causes happiness; deliverance from oppression brings the joy of God.

Mercy is defined as God's deserved favor. When we do a job and at the end collect the salary we deserve, if the person who commissioned the work does not pay us, that individual is someone without mercy. But if we work for God, we will always receive the retribution we deserve because He is merciful. He who prays, as David did, always receives an answer. The heart is the depository of emotions, and God uses it to brighten the lives of His children with the grace of salvation. Grace, which is what provides salvation, is God's undeserved gift to humankind because no human being is worthy to receive it since we are all sinners. It can only be ascribed to us through Jesus, who is the facilitator of that grace through the shedding of His precious and holy blood on the cross of Calvary for the forgiveness of our sins.

The most intimate and universal forms of expression of human feelings are music, singing, and poetry. David dominated all three: "I will sing unto the Lord, because he hath dealt bountifully with me." By singing, we promulgate our thoughts, feelings, and moods. The motive of David's music, songs, and poetry was not a break of love or a mournful cry or a war song. His song announced the deeds of Jehovah, who had done him good. Let us praise Jehovah for what He has done. Let us adore Him for who He is and exalt Him for all the good He has done for us.

PSALM 15

The main idea of the religious mentality of the people of Israel was that God dwelled in the tabernacle, and His power operated exclusively in relation to them. For the Israelites, the composition of society was limited to two groups, the chosen people (them) and the Gentiles (the other people). This concept continued in force until the apostle Paul, in Ephesians 2:14, expressed the social equality provided by Jesus's sacrifice: "For he is our peace, who hath made both one (Jews [the elect] and Gentiles [the separated]), and hath broken down the middle wall of partition between us." Moreover, the only ones who could inhabit the temple at that time were the priests of the tribe of Levi, so how could anyone else inhabit the temple if not a priest or descendant of Levi? Jehovah questions, "Lord, who shall abide in thy tabernacle? Who shall dwell in the holy hill? They were not literal concepts of dwelling in the temple but an exhortation to transform the popular idiosyncrasy, the religious ritual of the temple and the customs of the nation, into a spiritual worship that would allow living in close communion with God.

Dwelling in the tabernacle and dwelling on its holy mountain are two aspects of the same act. The tabernacle means protection (militant church), and the holy mountain represents communion (triumphant church). The tabernacle was placed in the middle of the camp so that Jehovah's presence would protect everyone equally and be seen from any angle and feel His presence.

These two questions can be summed up in one: Who can qualify to draw near to God? Luke 18:18 says, "And a certain ruler asked him, saying, Good Master, what shall I do to inherit eternal life?" And the answer is: Only Jesus has enough merit to be in the presence of God, and through Him, we can be in Jehovah's house, enjoying protection and communion with God. David, though he had no knowledge of Jesus's ministry to come, by revelation of the Spirit was announcing it here.

The Israelites had three fundamental barriers that prevented them from drawing near to God: the Law, which condemned them; the sacrifices, which did not exonerate; and themselves, who were rebels. The first thing necessary to solve a problem is to identify it and recognize it. The two questions in the first verse show this first step, and the answers begin to manifest themselves in the second verse: "He that walketh uprightly, and worketh righteousness, and speaketh the truth in his heart." "Uprightly" is the cohesion between what we speak and what we do; the veracity of the ministry depends on personal testimony. You must practice what you preach. We must show that we are convinced of what we teach by applying it in life. "And worketh righteousness," means not to apply our opinions based on the experiences we have lived, which are relative and they vary according to the circumstances, time, and place where they occurred. A child, a young person, or an adult does not think the same; an Asian, an African, or a European does not behave the same because their needs and realities of life, place, and circumstances are not the same. Instead, true justice is to apply God's commandments, which are absolute and do not vary according to circumstances, times, or places. What is written in the Word of God says, means, and has the same sense in all places and cultures, does not change according to circumstances, or deviate with the passage of time. God's justice does not get adapted to meet political, social, or economic demands. It always remains unshakable and, therefore, is the most effective rule for evaluating humankind's spiritual behaviors.

"And speaketh the truth in his heart," refers to righteousness, something that is done from us toward others (horizontal relationship). But the truth of the heart works from within toward God (vertical relationship). We have the capacity to appear what we are not in front of people, but we will never be able to hide our true intentions, thoughts, and attitudes in front of God, who scrutinizes hearts. Our intimate, personal attitude before God is more important than our public behaviors because what we do socially may be wrong or misinterpreted. But God will always rightly value our sincere attitudes toward Him. Private times of prayer should be honest and reflect the true feelings that motivate our actions. A heart that speaks truth is a regenerated heart.

Verse 3: He that backbiteth not with his tongue, nor doeth evil to his neighbour, not taketh up a reproach against his neighbour. The main characteristic a believer in Christ must have is discretion. This must determine the topic, extent, and quality of the conversations in which we participate because what we say has a permanent impact on the feelings of the listener and the person alluded to. We must be careful about the attitudes we praise in our comments so as not to incite inappropriate behaviors.

Slander is not always deliberately lying about someone to harm them. It also can be distorting the meaning of the facts to divert perceptions about someone or something from the positive to the negative. For example, when a person financially helps someone in need, and the ill-intentioned say that he or she did not do it out of kindness or mercy but out of pride and vanity. Slander not only destroys people's images and morals, it also tries to overshadow good results by creating frustration that destroys good intentions. Slander is perversity, so a Christian should not practice it so as not to do harm to his neighbor because to harm a person is to harm God.

The most constant of our feelings should be to serve as a help and blessing. The goodness of the kingdom of heaven must abound on earth through our godly and charitable actions toward those in our circles of influence. Christian character must be shaped by the nine characteristics of the fruit of the Spirit (Galatians 5:22, 23), which are the qualities Jesus Christ taught us during His earthly ministry. This distinctive character places us in a spiritual point of view, giving us the ability to see behind every action the one who really provokes them, the devil. We can then act and respond against the one who commits the damage and thus not taketh up a reproach and make accusations against the innocent neighbor. Spiritual vision is not guessing the future but understanding the spiritual influences that move behind reality.

Verse 4: In whose eyes a vile person is contemned; but the honoureth them that fear the Lord. He that sweareth to his own hurt, and changeth not. The only way to know what is wrong is to know what is right. The subconscious process of comparing the elements that make up the surrounding environment began when Adam and Eve ate the fruit of the tree of the knowledge of good and evil. In addition to knowing the good, they could now begin to know the evil. From that moment on, things were valued equivalently and appreciated differently in big and small, ugly, and pretty, useful and useless, good and bad. This pattern of thought as an innate defect in human nature, comparatively analyzes all the information received to classify it into the three known categories: good, regular, or bad. This ability to interpret appearances, events, and behaviors using preestablished concepts and principles, when submitted under biblical precepts, allows us to detect human feelings that do not manifest naturalness of God's love. The rejection of these manifestations is not moved by deliberate hatred of the person but as a rejection of evil and harmful manifestations that harm others. Those who wish to please God must forgive the wicked but reject wickedness. Obviously, those who reject evil love good. Therefore, they honor those who fear Jehovah. We know that circumstances and conditions change with time, people, and situations. Because of this, the oaths we have taken in the past may not be so appropriate in the present. But they have already been made and must be faced as they are, without changing the words, committed. God will honor our faithfulness.

Verse 5: He that putteth not out his money to usury, nor taketh reward against the innocent. He that doeth these things shall never be moved. Money is not bad in itself. Rather, it is the love of money that provokes the greed that can cause the believer to depart from faith. During times of economic scarcity, it is not fair to lend money with interest and make a profit. The right thing to do is to help financially with our resources to serve as a blessing. God does not supply us to make us rich; He does so to help us be a channel of relief by helping others. When someone in need cries out for help, God moves us to extend our hands to him. Selfishness and greed are not ingredients of the character of a good Christian. "Nor taketh reward against the innocent." Let us think about this. How many injustices do we know of but do not denounce because they do not harm us directly? We must reject any deviation from justice by defending fair positions that respect God's commandments.

"He that doeth these things shall never be moved."

This psalm is a teaching to find the way to heaven, exhorting us to achieve that purpose by walking in holiness and honesty. Injustice, deceit, defamation, and selfishness should never be part of how we deal with our neighbors.

PSALM 16

Verse 1 tells us the greatest manifestation of faith is confident surrender. Human existence, analyzed from an antagonistic point of view, is a confrontation of opposites. To live is to defy death; to rise is to overcome the resistance of the law of gravity that draws us downward; the love that unites is opposed to the hatred that separates; going north is the opposite of going south and different from going east or west. Any decision we make will always be in opposition to another related possibility. Dependence on God is directly proportional to the need that overwhelms us.

When David was pressed by a crisis, he had to take urgent action to resolve it. A wide range of options were in front of him: flee and abandon everything, give up and lose everything, defend himself depending on his strength, or surrender to fate and be resigned to endure anything that happened. But David had one resource that confronted all others—turning to Jehovah of the hosts, winner in battles. Those who have had revelation of God's existence know where to cry out. David decided to put his life in to Jehovah's purpose, following the spiritual thought pattern of faith: If I entrust my defense, assurance, and victory in the mighty hands of my redeemer, he will keep me and deliver me from all evil. The decision to go against all human choices, to rely on God's power, is the safest route we can take. Keep me, O God, because in You I have trusted. It is a clamor of mercy to God and a war cry for the enemy. This is an expression of double effect: If we trust in God, he keeps us; and if he keeps us, we can be confident. The world is ruled by divine spiritual forces that control human actions. And if we fervently cry out to those higher forces, they will make human deeds happen for our well-being. The moment we present our cry before Jesus as a plea, the protection that God offers us will have the dimension of eternal salvation.

In verse 2 we see that the perfect place to proclaim that Jehovah is God is in the soul, and the right approach to manifest divine majesty begins in the elements that make it up: will, intelligence, and feelings. The will controls decisions within established rules, and intelligence provides the appropriate conditions according to the circumstances and feelings to balance the manifestation of the results. Everyone who confesses his or her sins, dangers, and hopes recognizes first, guilt; second, fears; third, purposes.

Placing our pasts, presents, and futures in the hands of God is to create the perfect complement for the objectives we intend to achieve in life. There are two spiritual scopes: society, where everything is bad and goes for the worse; and that of God, where everything is good and continues for the better. Where we place our desires, hopes, and actions determines the results. Choosing the right place does not depend on reasoning but on faith. According to logic, the right thing to do is to take care of ourselves because God cannot be seen. According to faith, we must seek God because He is the rewarder of those who seek Him, convinced that He exists. The statements of the soul are not to be heard by human ears but by divine sensitivity. The sure cry, "You are my Lord," into heavenly mercy as a seal of acceptance and surrender that moves the spiritual currents, bringing to us the flow of peace that defeats all insecurities. One's desire must be for God, that everything be focused on His provision. Outside of it, nothing is convenient. The supreme source of blessing is God.

Verse 3: Holy is the antonym of sin. Before the disobedience of Adam and Eve, because sin had not entered humanity the idea of saint—as we understand it today—was not known. Humanity was pure. But after the fall, the concept of sin appeared. It then became necessary to conceptualize holiness as a spiritual resource to reverse the sinful process in humankind. Hence, the word *holy* has the meaning of consecrated or set apart for God. The opportunity to be holy on earth is so that we can become glorified souls in heaven. Contrary to what is commonly thought, the saints are not those on the altars but those who walk the world, preaching the gospel with tenacity and boldness. Those are the honest, those who teach by example and witness, those who give themselves to God by living the faith of Jesus. Integrity is building an indissoluble core through the words and actions that define our personalities. These are examples of divine gratification.

When we please God, we enjoy His favor, grace, and mercy. There is no greater beatitude than to receive the retribution of God's satisfaction. Even if we feel good because life has favored us, we may sometimes behave badly because we have turned our backs on God. The intentions and directions of our actions play a significant role in the positions we reach in the spiritual appreciation we receive from God. On many occasions, we wonder why something we did went wrong if we did it right. Well, what happened is that we got the result of an incorrectly designed process. Perhaps the intention, direction, or frequency of action did not accord with God's plans. It is important to act on the flow of divine will and purposes since nothing happens if it is not first approved on the heavenly throne.

Verse 4 can be viewed as relating to science. In the age we live in, science has found an explanation for all the phenomena that manifest in nature, the atmosphere, the sea, the land— in all the known realms. But it has been unable to find an explanation for miracles. When supernatural effects occurred in biblical times, human communities erected symbols of objects and animals to beg for protection from the inclement weather and consequences of what might or was happening. Basically, the ignorance and lack of protection from the unknown of the first human societies led to the origin of idolatry. But Satan, the devil, included it in his strategies for separating humankind from God by proposing other comfortable, easy-to-follow prototypes to divert us from the one true God, Jehovah.

Idolatry leads to painful separation from God, causing the greatest sadness that can afflict the soul. To serve idols is to dig the tomb of the Spirit, where the hopes of salvation will be buried. Even mentioning idols' names clouds the purity of holiness. The only libation of blood that God accepts is the one Jesus shed on the cross. Physical pain is relieved with medicines and treatments. But spiritual pain is only relieved by the presence of the Holy Spirit in our lives.

Verse 5 proclaims the reward of those who choose Jehovah as their defender and protector is enormous and fruitful. One's portion is the fertile ground for the seed scattered by the sower to grow; the Promised Land, where milk and honey flow; and the blessed church, where the power of God is poured out. One's inheritance is the presence of God, the saving sacrifice of Jesus, and the ministration of the Holy Spirit. The cup is the precious, holy, divine blood of Jesus, who shed on the cross for our redemption and forgiveness of our sins. There is nothing more beautiful and prosperous than the inheritance that Jehovah has given us. We must delight in it, and praise Him for His provision of trust and security. The satisfaction we experience thanks to God's protection must be manifested with joy and rejoicing that the world be infected with the euphoria of belonging to supreme things that magnify and perfect us as people. God's sublimity must not go unnoticed before the eyes of the world.

Verse 7 teaches that the relationship that unites conscience and advice is analysis and decision. Consciousness, based on its code of values, processes the information to account for results and evaluates them properly. When this process is monitored following the principles established by God in the Bible, confirmation takes place that grows the character, scope, and fruit of the required purpose.

A notorious detail of God's unsurpassed wisdom is that it is available to all thanks to its expressive clarity and simple understanding. The language of God is not scientific but spiritual. Therefore, it is not a matter of intelligence but of search and consecration. God's school is the only way to reach wisdom. We do not know why, but we do know how. The secret is not to ask, just to act.

Verse 8: If we put Jehovah in front, He will lead us in safe ways and will be the best protective shield we can count on in any battle. What we fly in the vanguard, flag and banner, is affirmation of who we are and where we are going, and what defines us. It announces what we are looking for, and where we intend to find it. When God goes to the bow of the ship, He divides the waters to open routes to new destinations and protects our flanks so the enemy's fire darts do not pierce the spiritual armor that covers us. The right hand is the strong hand in which we trust and deliver the hardest tasks; it is an arm of power, and nothing stops it. If we take refuge in Jesus, we will be surrounded by the weapons of the Holy Spirit that thwart the attacks of the enemy. If God is in front and at our right hands, nothing can take us away from the luminous path that leads to heaven.

Verse 9 and 10 shares the indescribable and immense satisfaction that floods the believers' lives as we see God's hand working wonders for our well-being and favor. Our hearts rejoice so much when we feel the presence of the Holy Spirit! Our souls rejoice so much with the flow of divine power! There is nothing more comforting than the security of knowing that against all odds, things will be fine. Joy comes from the promise that we do not belong to death but to life, and our flesh is destined for glorification and not putrefaction.

When the people of Israel were camped in front of the Promised Land, preparing to cross the Jordan River, Jehovah said to Joshua (Joshua 1:13), "Remember the word which Moses

Also, in Jewish tradition, *Sheol* (Hades in the New Testament) was where the dead went. However, they retained a conscious spiritual state because, although they believed there was a life beyond natural life, they had not received the concept of life resurrected in the presence of God, which Jesus revealed long after his earthly ministry. Sheol was divided into two parts: the place of torment, where those who died in injustice received their punishments; and Abraham's bosom, where those who had died in the righteousness of the Law enjoyed their rewards (Luke 16:19–26). Here was where Jesus descended while in the tomb, before He was resurrected to present himself as the Messiah to those who waited on God for the day of redemption (Ephesians 4:8–10; 1 Peter 3:18–20) and to preach to them the gospel of salvation so that they could be taken to heaven along with Him on the day of resurrection. God's rest that was not achieved in Canaan is fulfilled in Jesus because He is superior to Moses, Joshua, David, and everyone and everything, being the apostle and high priest of our profession (Hebrews 3:1), and the great High Priest who pierced the heavens (Hebrews 4:14).

Verse 11 talks about looking to heaven. It is the most effective method of seeing on earth. The human being looks at everything but sees nothing. Why? Because reality is not what we perceive but the forces that provoke it. To look at something is the act of observing; to see is the act of receiving the vision. When God shows us how to separate physical reality from spiritual reality, the revelation of the path that leads to eternal life begins. Jehovah does not give us life to walk the path; He shows us the path to attain life. This path is traveled, fulfilling the requirements of the believer's way of life that are only achieved when guided by the Holy Spirit.

We exist in a life that encompasses several facets of behavior that, when advancing along the path of life shown by God, become the definitions of Christian character. The main aspects in projecting the personality of a follower of Christ are repentance, consecration, faithfulness, holiness, and testimony. Repentance manifests itself in the change of attitude when we begin to deny ourselves to sin. We see consecration in the change of activities when we change interests. Fidelity—faithfulness—becomes noticeable when we follow new patterns of behavior. We demonstrate holiness in character as we seem to become more and more like Christ. And when we witness, give testimony, is the development of God's work in personal relationships.

God's presence is the contact we establish with Him through interactions between our spiritual sensitivities and the influence of the Holy Spirit. This communion produces an anointing effect that infects everything around us and saturates the environment through ministering. Anointing is how God makes others feel by using us. The presence of God is a possession that belongs to us by right of faith. It satisfies all the needs of the soul with unparalleled joy, and we can rest confident and secure. In His presence, we belong and participate in Him.

The locations of our relationships determine the goals we follow, the directions we take, and the results we get. Coordinating faith with biblical postulates ensures fullness of joy, manifesting the scope and meaning of feeling God's presence by nourishing our spirits to unite us closely with Him. Joy is the intimate spiritual rejoicing in the sacrifices God has allowed us to make in His work. Joy is not pleasure but commitment and surrender because God always blesses us for thinking about providing someone else with what He gives us. Selfishness stops God's provision; altruism accelerates the flow of the Holy Spirit to meet needs we may face. Delight surpasses all measures of satisfaction, plunging us into a state of peace and happiness only God can give when we feel the security provided by entrusting Him with all our vicissitudes. There is nothing more exciting than resting in Jehovah. But the real delights will be enjoyed eternally at the right hand of God, from which no one can separate us because Jesus Christ placed us there through faith, consecration, and sanctification.

PSALM 20

Living while trying to reach the peace of God is the most conflictive mission we can undertake. It happens this way, not because of us or God, but because of the opposition of evil forces that use all means to hinder divine plans. In this way, we can say that the spiritual life of the believer is under permanent attack from Satan.

The Lord's work is always difficult, but God makes it easy. If a businessperson opens a bar, it is filled from the first day. If a pastor tries to stablish a new church, it takes time to form a congregation and often fails to do so. But the satisfaction of preaching the gospel of Jesus Christ far outweighs all difficulties and failures. In the days of our sorrows and sadness, when betrayals hurt us, when we are victims of human injustices, we pray to Jehovah to listen to our pleas and respond with fair judgments on our causes, always declaring with faith that the best is yet to come. There is no complaint that God does not hear. Nor are there regrets that He does not attend. The blind Bartimaeus cried out to Jesus in faith saying,

Jesus, thou Son of David, have mercy on me, defying those who rebuked him not to do so, but the Lord heard him and stood still calling him: What wilt thou that I should do unto thee? And Bartimaeus, throwing out his garment, which was all he possessed, came to Jesus, and said to him: Lord, that I might receive my sight. And Jesus said unto him, go thy way; thy faith hath made thee whole. And immediately he receives his sight and followed Jesus in the way. (Mark 10:46–52)

Bartimaeus had a life of conflict. Being blind in biblical times was far worse than we can imagine today. He was forced to live in the streets, begging. No one helped him because it meant a burden. He was despised because physical defects were considered God's punishment for sin, and therefore, he was obligated to stay on the side of the road. But Jesus came, and Bartimaeus cried out to him with the magic words that move God's compassion: "Have mercy on me!" God listened to him, answered him, and healed him.

We face today, tomorrow, and always a multitude of conflicts. We are criticized and disdained as people and as believers. But during tribulation, we must understand that Jesus is constantly able to listen, respond, and resolve our conflicts. We just need to cry out, "Have mercy on me," and Jehovah will hear the heartbreaking weeping of the soul and pour all His comfort and relief upon us with unparalleled love. Trust God, and He will do.

God's name is not just three letters forming a word but actions creating power. The name of God is above every name and generates spiritual anointing that makes everything possible. In biblical times, due to the scarcity of lexicons of ancient languages, names were not a unique word to identify something or someone, which they have become. Rather, they were words that expressed an idea that formed a phrase describing an event. For example, Cain, which means, "I have gotten a man from the Lord" (Genesis 4:1), or Jabez, which means, "Because I bare him with sorrow" (1 Chronicles 4:9). In Jehovah's case, the Israelites avoided mentioning His proper name and had several words that expressed a broader concept to refer to Him, including, Yahweh-Jired, the Lord will provide; Yahweh-Rapha, the Lord who heals;

Yahweh-Nisi, the Lord is my flag; Yahweh-Shalom, the Lord is our peace; and Yahweh-Elohim, the Lord is God. But God's personal name is Yahweh, which categorically means, I Am who I Am; and his surname is Elohim, which means God. So, during these ancient times, names expressed the origin and purpose of each thing, place, or person. The indication in the verse that the name of Jacob's God defends you, is the request and declaration that I am the one who is God—with all knowledge, right, and authority—listening to your plea in the hour of conflict to intervene and impose the plan that was always dedicated for this moment. I am who I am, God of times, history, and future, and I will fight for you and defend you against all your enemies so that my will may be fulfilled among the men as a testimony of my power. The mention of the patriarch Jacob is a reminder of Jehovah's protection upon him throughout his pilgrimage on earth, saving him from enemies, persecutions, wars, and famines. That same saving and merciful power will be forever with His children. God continues defending His people and will do so until He returns to raise up His church.

The second verse says, "Send thee help from the sanctuary and strengthen thee out of Zion." These are the two holy places from where help comes to overcome trials and tribulations. The sanctuary is the heavenly throne, where Jesus is seated and interceding for us. Zion is the church where prayers for protection are raised. The first and fundamental help descends from heaven along with the power of the Holy Spirit. The second reaches us because of the commitment and worship in the church here on earth. The sending of divine aid joins us while we walk with God, and what God sends, no one can stop. Jehovah has no doubt that He will sustain us. Therefore, in us there should be no doubt of His protection because He is, in Himself, the provider of all things.

Verse 3 points to the reality that there are sacrifices God does not accept because they do not meet His rules or are not offered by faith but by obligation and custom. Faith has a key role in everything we do for God. In reference to sacrifices and offerings, what we believe is worth more than what we do. We must remember that "without faith, it is impossible to please Him" (Hebrews 11:6). In this regard, what Jehovah remembers and blesses is one's spiritual disposition and what we do with it, not the quantity or quality of what we deliver to the altar. The believer can recognize that his or her sacrifices have been received and accepted by experiencing the powerful presence of the Holy Spirit that drives the believer to serve, worship, and praise the supreme Creator.

Let us give our wonderful God the satisfaction of seeing us bring to His throne the best of sacrifices and offerings—our lives—in obedience and holiness. Let us adore Him with the fervor He deserves.

Verse 4 shows that giving is an intrinsic attitude of God's nature. In the divinity, we find that his greatest dedication is to pour the riches of heavenly treasures upon our earthly needs. Everything we own has been provided in this way. But God's giving depends on the desire of the heart. The Bible says in James 4:3, "Ye ask, and receive not, because ye ask amiss, that ye may consume it upon your lusts." Prayer must focus on the attainment of spiritual purposes of the kingdom of God, the church, and the strengthening of faith in the believer. It should never seek to achieve individual, social, political, or economic advantages, riches, or benefits.

God is for everyone, not just for some. We must not be walls that contain the blessing; we must be channels through which the flow of the Spirit runs freely. From Him, we will receive what is necessary when the desire of our hearts accord with His will. It is a matter of attunement and spiritual communication.

The apostle Paul wrote in Romans 8:16 that "The Spirit itself beareth witness with our spirit, that we are the children of God"; and in Romans 8:26, "Likewise the Spirit also helpeth our infirmities; for we know not what we should pray for as we ought: but the Spirit itself maketh intercession for the saints according to the will of God."

The Word of God is the best counselor we can consult, and the one who is guided by it will never stumble. Biblical counsel is the only one that will be fulfilled in the divine determination to do His work through the effort of His children. Whatever is not part of the godly plan will never happen. That is why we must seek to do what the Bible manifests. Applying good advice from God is a sign of spiritual maturity. Our Lord Jesus Christ declared it this way: "And now, O Father, glorify thou me with thine own self with the glory which I had with thee before the world was" (John 17:5). And the apostle Paul, "I have fought a good fight, I have finished my course, I have kept the faith" (2 Timothy 4:7). These are the supreme prizes of victories when God's Word is fulfilled in our personal lives.

The fifth verse speaks of joy for the salvation, exalting God's name for the victories, and God granting us our requests. First, the joys provided by human satisfaction are euphoric emotional states of unmeasured pleasure that end when the external stimulation that causes them stops influencing our sensory systems. Personal emotions fade away with the passage of time because everything related to humanity is temporary; it does not remain. Moods are fickle, feelings variable, and emotional responses depend on what happens around individuals as they relate to the environment to which they are socially exposed.

Another aspect to consider is that joy is often caused by incorrect reasons. Therefore, being cheerful does not necessarily imply being in a convenient feeling. Ill-founded joy is harmful.

On the contrary, rejoicing in salvation puts feelings into an inner emotional dimension that nourishes the spirit in the fullness of the joy of submitting the natural to the supernatural. This joy, the result of the Holy Spirit's victory over the sin that overwhelms us, is not expressed with applause, laughter, dances, or feasts. Rather, expression comes through dedication, consecration, obedience, and holiness in the activities we perform, reflecting the joy that invades us due to the assurance that God is involved in our affairs. Being saved is not an emotion or autosuggestion. It is a conscious reaction to the presence of a new spiritual reality that floods us with higher life expectations than we had previously. Salvation is the relief of knowing you are on the right path to the best destination for the human soul, the presence of God. Then we will sing a song of joy that will raise God's victory over sin. We will be the army, the fortress, and the refuge of the Highest, raising the Word of God as the weapon of our redemptions. And Jehovah, exalted and sublime, in the goodness of His mercy will grant all our petitions.

Jehovah's anointed ones are well cared for, and their salvations are assured. The first anointed are the people of Israel, who received the Law, prophecies, and promises. The second anointed is Jesus, who satisfied all the requirements of the Law, fulfilled the prophecies, and secured the promises for the currently anointed ones who worship God in Spirit and truth. Salvation descends from heaven because God hears the moans of His people on earth. In the perfection of His holiness, the necessary help is always available to be poured out abundantly in victories and blessings in the fulfillment of His promises. "With saving power": Salvation is the energy that produces the change of nature that places us in the new spiritual position for those who do not walk according to the flesh, but according to the Spirit (Romans 8:1). It ends by pointing out, "from his right hand," which highlights the ability, precision, and perfection of time, methods, and results. God's right hand is the emancipatory hand that breaks the chains and liberates the oppressed.

Trust is a way of depending on what we assume will answer our needs or will be available when required. The processes, systems, and individuals outside divine protection count their strengths and possibilities based on available resources. Governments trust their armies, armies in their soldiers, and soldiers in their weapons. But when separated from Jehovah, there is no complete victory, even if one wins the battle, because winning is not only to defeat the enemy but to achieve peace. And for that, the enemy must surrender to the superiority of God's power.

Confidence apart from God means waiting in uncertainty. But united with Him, expectation becomes faith, which is total assurance that it will happen according to the divine plan revealed in the Bible, which we are following. Because of this, the believer must place his or her anxieties in the guidance of the Holy Spirit to be led to the encounter and a relationship with Jesus. The history of battles fought in the power of God builds a trajectory of security that extends in the face of new difficulties by announcing the next victories. Jehovah's name announces triumph, peace, and security. This is the ideological concept of faith that should dominate spiritual life and Christian ministry. The name above every name—King of Kings, Lord of Lords, Prince of peace, God with us—will be by our sides until the end of days. Therefore, the one who perseveres to the end will be saved. Our encounters with God are not single points but uninterrupted lines of blessings. The Bible teaches us in Deuteronomy 8:18, "But thou shalt remember the Lord thy God: for it is he that giveth thee power to get wealth, that he may establish his covenant which he sware unto thy fathers, as it is this day." To remember Jehovah is to remember the covenant made through the blood of Jesus Christ for the forgiveness of the sins of humankind. It covers us and cleanses us of guilt so that we can be in the most holy and powerful presence of the heavenly Father.

The great difficulty of planning the future using human accounting and reasoning patterns is that they do not work. The surest way to fail is not to listen to the voice of the Holy Spirit. The coordination of what we do with God's designs is the only possibility we have of taking our projects to completion. So those who follow His advice will resist every attack of the enemy with courage, and nothing can bring us down. Getting up is not difficult if we lean on Jesus, and standing is not exhausting when his power sustains us.

The psalm ends triumphantly by declaring, "Save, Lord; let the King hear us when we call." One of the determining characteristics of the deity is that He reveals success before strife. Jehovah let Abraham know what He would do with him before leaving Ur of the Chaldeans in Mesopotamia (Genesis 12:1–3). When the angel of the Lord appeared to Moses in the burning bush on Mount Horeb, he was told that he would deliver the people of Israel from slavery in Egypt (Exodus 3:2). Joshua received the mission (Joshua 1:2) and the annunciation of victory (Joshua 1:5) before crossing the Jordan River. When God entrusts us with a mission, he also sends the instructions on how to develop it, along with the provision to accomplish it. God does not intend to make us look ridiculous; He makes us more than victors. "Save, Lord," is not a desperate plea amid the desolation of defeat. Rather, it is an order of combat, certain of the victorious outcome, announced by Jehovah to the armies that the King of heaven will hear the day we call Him. The divine ear is attentive to the cry of its children; nothing escapes its attention and response. Before the cry of repentance of the sinner, the saving holiness of God comes to his aid immediately. To God be all glory and honor.

PSALM 23

"The Lord is my shepherd, I shall not want." This does not mean we will have everything but that we will be able to fight for it. It does not refer to possessions but to decisions. That we will seek everything we need with the Lord's strength, because if Jehovah shepherds us, there will never be a lack of a purpose to fulfill in His plans of optimal spiritual development. Being shepherded by Jehovah is the most wonderful experience a human being can have. He seeks, finds, and attends us directly with all love, patience, and consideration. He leads us on the path of redemption. He who has God does not need anything else.

But Jehovah will not *do* the task; He will *teach* us the duties and responsibilities necessary to perform it. The pastor guides, trains, and commissions the workers for the harvest. This verse personalizes the divine pastorate, pointing to it as something individual. Jehovah, God of the universe, has deigned to attend and sustain me personally. Jesus, the good Shepherd (John 10:11), carries us on His shoulders like beloved sheep. But we must adopt a spiritual sheep attitude to receive the protection of the heavenly shepherd.

The position with respect to God is defining as to what we will receive from Him. This second verse speaks of where Jehovah is to place us. First, "He maketh me to lie down in green pastures," which are by no means weak or fragile, but excellent and exquisite. They are where the presence of the Spirit dwells, preparing the food of His children with the best ingredients for spiritual health. The rest that God has in store for us is not inactivity but an abundant life in His presence.

Second, "He leadeth me beside the still waters." The waters, although never at rest, provide a sense of tranquility, and their proximity announces freshness and vitality. Life is impossible without water. That is why Jesus is Himself living water (John 7:38) that gives life. The waters do not repeat; they are renewed. Thus, we must constantly renew ourselves in the process of growth as people of faith.

The emphasis of this psalm is on the protection, provision, and security the shepherd provides to the sheep. In verse 3, he speaks of the need to comfort the soul, where the characteristics that define the human being originate: intelligence, will, and feelings. Intelligence will be comforted with wisdom from on high; the will shall be strengthened with the power of the Holy Spirit; and feelings will be regenerated in the new birth, transforming us into new creatures. The soul comforted by God is an impregnable fortress. Comforting, in addition to restoration, strengthens one to continue, encouraging one to persevere, and pushing one to move forward.

Jehovah could have decided to compare His people to a herd of fierce lions, aggressive tigers, or unstoppable elephants. But in His immense wisdom, He compared them to helpless sheep. Why? Although it may seem absurd, it is not. Sheep have peculiar characteristics that, in their relationship with the shepherd, show useful teachings for those who want to please God. The sheep have a very limited sense of direction and location, causing them to be easily lost if they stray only a short distance from the shepherd and the flock. Just like us. This defect also causes the sheep not to know how to go on their own to places where there are fresh pastures and food for them, making them dependent on the shepherd for their guidance and subsistence. Just like us. To be sheep of Jehovah's flock means to depend totally on the good shepherd (John 10:11, 14) and maintaining a communion through obedience to Him. That is why the verse goes on to affirm, "He leadth me in the paths of righteousness for his name's sake."

A spiritual analogy about this reality is found in the New Testament, when the disciples asked our Lord Jesus, "Who is the greatest in the kingdom of heaven?" He called a child and answered them, "Verily I say unto you, except ye be converted, and become as little children, ye shall not enter into the kingdom of heaven" (Matthew 18:1–5). There is a similarity in nature between a child and a sheep. Both are unable to locate, feed, and survive on their own. Sheep depend on the shepherd; children depend on their parents. If we interrupt dependence on our pastor and Father, we perish.

"In the paths of righteousness": This guide of the good shepherd are paths chosen and approved expressly for one's comfort, relief, and benefit. "For his name's sake": Honor His name, which is above all names. God cares for His children because we are His special creations by conversion, conviction, and consecration, all revealing His character and showing His power. As children, we must love God the Father as a sign of respect, praise, and worship because He takes care of our security, protection, and guidance.

From the trust in the comfort, supply, and protection that are activated with the power of the Holy Spirit, who assists us, a cry of victory is born that evokes eternal salvation: "Yea, though I walk through the valley of the shadow of death, I will fear no evil, for thou art with me." No matter the threats, the dangers, the enemy attacks, fear never has the right to possess or weaken our spiritual attitudes of consecration and perseverance in the faith of Jesus Christ.

This verse does not assume the possibility of defeat or death but the assurances of life and victory. Romans 8:37 says, "Nay, in all these things we are more than conquerors through him that loved us." All human beings will experience physical death one day, but spiritual death is optional. Those who reject Jehovah, believing that physical death is the end of everything, are unaware that a tormented eternity awaits them outside the kingdom of heaven. But for those who assume Jehovah as their shepherd, physical death represents the liberation of the corrupt body to enter the incorruptible spiritual life in the heavenly Jerusalem. God's sheep can face the battles of faith with courage and decisiveness because we have nothing to lose and much to gain because the shepherd is with us. When Jehovah attends events, He ensures success. The plans, strategies, and tactics we put into practice only achieve spiritual achievements of blessing if they implement the divine will.

The confirmation of what was said above is defined by the final sentence of the verse: "Thy rod and Thy staff they comfort me." Each trade has its specific tools, designed appropriately to fulfill the different tasks related to its functions. In this case, the tools of the sheepherder are the rod and the staff. The rod is a wooden stake, the size of a saber or sword, which was tied to the waist. In those times, it was most likely a strong and resistant tree branch used to defend the flock from the attacks of wild beasts. The staff was also a wooden rod, but it was longer and had an inverted U shape that served as a hook to guide and keep the sheep united in the fold. For us, the rod represents the weapon of combat, the Bible, and the staff is the obedience and holiness that guides us and holds us together in the faith of Jesus Christ. Jehovah, our shepherd, has given us the weapons of His trade so that we may continue the work He began with Jesus, the good shepherd, who came to save the Lord's flock.

The fifth verse teaches five things from God:

1) Provision: Table dressings

2) Communion: In front of me.

3) Protection: In the presence of my tormentors.

4) Power: God anoint my head with oil.

5) Rejoicing: My glass is overflowing.

The victories God bestows upon us are celebrated in style with abundance (table), anointing (oil), and joy (cup). There is no better host than Jehovah. He organizes the biggest of all parties. As a father, He seeks the best food for His children. As a shepherd, He seeks the best pasture for His sheep. And in His Son, Jesus, Jehovah provides us with the best of gifts: forgiveness of our sins and salvation. A celebration of such magnitude changes the sense of human perspectives from an earthly point of view to a heavenly expectation. Really, we are much more than fortunate to be sheep of the divine shepherd because we enjoy infinite provision ("I shall not want"), freedom from fear ("I will fear no evil"), and an assured eternity ("I will dwell in the house of the Lord forever").

The social idiosyncrasies of the ancient peoples of the Middle East included the idea that caring carefully for guests and strangers brought blessing (Deuteronomy 10:19; Hebrews 13:2). Therefore, showing and having an attitude of welcome toward those in need overflows with blessings in our lives. The secret of having is to give, to be a channel of blessing. All who act in this way will see the goodness of God promised in verse 6 flood their realities: "Surely goodness and mercy shall follow me all the days of my life, and I will dwell in the house the house of the Lord forever." The word *certainly* declares that the truth, the amen, and the will of God are committed to us. Our well-being will undoubtedly descend from heaven. Good differs from mercy in that good is born in the will, and mercy is motivated by love. Good is concerned with the body, mercy with the spirit. This will endure, "all the days of my life." As our lives go on, this promise should be the real-time spiritual appraisal that sustains faith and the conviction that the pastor's assistance is assured. And not only in this part of heaven but also in eternity: "And I will dwell in the house of the Lord forever." The indissoluble bond of fidelity between the wayward sheep returned to the fold and the shepherd who lays down His life for it transcends the limitations of time, space, and matter into the divine dimension of salvific eternity.

PSALM 27

"The Lord is my light and my salvation; Who shall I fear?" Jehovah, light, and salvation have one thing in common: They have no human logical explanation. Jehovah exists; therefore, He is real, we feel His presence, and we are convinced that He works in the circumstances in which we live. But there is no way to conceptualize Him to show His origin, consistency, or composition. Light exists; it is real. We know that it is present because it illuminates the world. But there is no concise physical or chemical formula that teaches how it originates or what it is made of. Salvation exists; it is real. We know it is there because the Word of God reveals it clearly. But we cannot prove it because it defies all the rules of human knowledge. The impossibility of defining Jehovah, light, and salvation exists because they are divine, and divine things are impenetrable to the human mind and, therefore, are beyond the dimensions of time, space, and matter. They must be revealed by the Spirit of who ordered it to be that way. From the conviction of this reality, the challenging question arises, who shall I fear? If I belong to the One above all things, what can happen that represents a threat to me? There are infinite opportunities that will create disadvantageous positions for us. There will be countless adverse moments. But Jehovah, the God who made light and designed salvation, will always be present as a protective shield, so there is no reason to fear.

"The Lord is the strength of my life; of whom shall I be afraid?" This quotation expresses the same concept but in a different aspect. Human strength lies in bones, muscles, and food. But the strength that comes from God consists in giving up our attitudes. Human strength and its might do not stop hatred, prevent attacks, or mitigate pain. Instead, they encourage it and lend themselves more to oppression than to liberation. The strength received from God develops the conviction that nothing and no one will be able to bend the faith. No obstacle will cause consecration to decline, and no circumstance will weaken the power of the Holy Spirit that we received as a reward for repentance and obedience.

"Of whom shall I be afraid?" Fear results from incapacity or ignorance. These two characteristics are derived from the absence of God in an individual's life. But when Jehovah assists us with His wisdom and teachings, the antidote is found in His sacred Word:

1) Incapacity: "Therefore I take pleasure in infirmities, in reproaches, in necessities, in persecutions, in distresses for Christ's sake: for when I am weak, then am I strong" (2 Corinthians 12:10).

2) Ignorance: "If any of you lack wisdom, let him ask of God, that giveth to all men liberally, and upbraideth not; and it shall be given him" (James 1:5).

From these fervent declarations of belonging and trust, a chant in crescendo toward victory begins. Effective vanguards need a powerful rearguard, which is precisely what we find here. We know that we will move safely on the paths that please God because we are supported by the expeditious purposes of carrying His Word: "Nay, in all these things we are more than conquerors through him that loved us" (Romans 8:37).

"When the wicked, even mine enemies and my foes, came upon me to eat up my flesh, they stumbled and fell." The worst and main enemies of the spiritual life of the believer are the flesh, society, and Satan, who, taking opportunity from the weaknesses of the flesh, pressures us with his hidden strategies of apparent benefits to separate us from obedience to the divine commandments. Nowadays, no secular institution responds to biblical interests and Christian moral principles. Our enemies, distressers, and evil ones are not horrible monsters with long horns and trident tails trying to annihilate us. Rather, they are liberalism, immorality, and atheism, which try to eliminate us as a spiritual influence within society, spreading false theories about the Christian faith, covering themselves under atheistic science, progress, and equality. But despite their apparent accomplishments, they will never be able to defeat God's anointed church on earth (Matthew 16:18).

The third verse does not speak of attack but of siege. The enemy army that comes against us camps, positions itself, presses, and waits. Its purpose is to weaken our strength and endurance to bend us out of tiredness, despair, and weariness. Corroding the spiritual tenacity of the believer is the main strategy of the adversary of souls because if he decrees a direct attack, he reveals his evil identity and loses the surprise effect. Satan's tactic is not explosion but implosion. To destroy the church from within, invading it with false theories, doctrines, and behaviors, thereby causing a process of worldliness in the activities and inner workings of the house of God. Because of this, the church must not yield to the roots of its principles of fear and fidelity to sacred scripture. In the eagerness to conquer the world, we cannot allow the world to conquer us. Those who come to Christ cannot bring the world with them; they must leave it behind. They must renounce their customs and abandon their ancient practices. The new spiritual nature that Jesus gives us is not compatible with the rules of society far from God. We are on earth but belong to heaven, and inevitably, at some point the encounter will be frontal. But we can be confident because Jehovah is our light and salvation.

Verse 4 discusses prayer. Prayer consists of two fundamental elements—petition and action—since nothing happens without an intention that seeks it and a force that produces it. The most effective way to cry out for what we need is to go out and find it sponsored by the faith that is sure God has already ordained it, and in due time, it will be fulfilled. The best of all prayers is to be the solution to the problem.

The second aspect that gives form and consistency to the prayer is the recipient, the claim, and its destiny. It is very important to direct our wishes to the right person, someone willing and able to help us. In spiritual matters of salvation, protection, and permanence, the only one who meets these three requirements is Jehovah, Creator of all that exists. Our prayers will be fulfilled exclusively if we address them to the exalted, majestic, and sublime heavenly recipient, who in addition to listening to them, pays attention and answers them. What we intend to achieve with our pleas must be consistent with the basic purposes of the divine spiritual essence, and we must commit our will to its fulfillment so that the destination we reach is the permanent stay in the presence of God.

When living as a guest in someone's house, it is required that one complies with the established discipline to please the host. The same is true for remaining in the house of Jehovah, which is not only heaven, but also the church and us as the temple of the Holy Spirit (1 Corinthians 6:19). The main spiritual conduct we must observe is love, from which we obtain the capacity to obey, implant, and display the qualities of the Christian character consecrated to remain and endure in the divine dwellings Jesus prepared for the children of God.

The next condition for being close to Him is humility, which does not refer to a certain social or economic level but to a character virtue. A person can be poor but proud; another can be rich and maintain humility. The direct result of a humble character is subjection to God's Word, goodness, service, and faithfulness because being humble is the indispensable condition in a person to obey. The privilege of beholding Jehovah's beauty deserves all the sacrifices we must make to achieve it. This contemplation produces ecstasy, surrender, and sublimation of spiritual perception. The new vision becomes the purpose of attaining the revelation of God's Word through the presence of the Holy Spirit in our lives. A new light illuminates us. New destinies await us: the temple of God, the heavenly dwelling place, and eternal life.

Verse 5 refers to the tabernacle built by Moses under the direction of Jehovah. It was the religious, political, and social center of the Israeli people. People met there to make important decisions and plan actions related to matters pertinent to the existence and direction of the nation, all led by God's inspired revelation. In the Jewish faith, the tabernacle was Jehovah's dwelling place, and from there His power, wisdom, goodness, and protection were manifested. Basically, the tabernacle for them represented salvation because they followed the logical reasoning that if it came from there, it was because it resided in that place. That is why this verse begins by declaring the blessing of being in Jehovah's house every day: "For in the time of trouble he shall hide me in his pavilion," for we are all safe in God's tabernacle. But blessings are never unique and limited; they are multiple and prolonged. So, He will hide us (put us to safety) in the secret (safest) place in His tabernacle (His divine temple), and upon a rock (Christ) He will put me up (the kingdom of heaven).

Verse 6 reads, "And now shall mine head be lifted up above mine enemies round about me (victory); Therefore, will I offer in his tabernacle sacrifices of joy (obedience); I will sing, yea, I will sing praises unto the Lord (worship)." Here we see a sample of the two-way road in the relationship with God. First, from Him to us. He gives us victory, facilitates obedience, and provokes worship. And second, from us to Him. We offer Him worship, obey His rules, and receive victory. We are complete in God, Christ, and the Holy Spirit. Humankind falls to pieces through guilt, but God rebuilds it with forgiveness.

Verse 7 tells us that no matter how well our personal, family, economic, or social affairs may go, everything we have prayed for is never enough. We always need to keep praying and crying out to God: "Hear, O Lord, when I cry with my voice." All the good we have is due to what we have prayed, and God provided. But we cannot trust ourselves because we think that because we already have it, we will never lose it. But we must persevere in the same attitude of prayer and devotion to preserve it.

"Have mercy also upon me and answer me." Mercy is supplying for love, providing for mercy, and giving with joy. Only God can do these three things to establish His existence, presence, and assistance. He will always exceed our expectations because He never subtracts or divides. He always adds and multiplies.

The next three verses are understood as a spiritual trident:

1) Verse 8: "Seek Jehovah, the best decision" (consecration). The heart, seen as a biological organ, propels blood flow in the body through the arteries and veins that make up the circulatory system. But this same heart, when identified as a spiritual element, understands the divine origin of life and is responsible for establishing communication and communion with the Creator for in God's plans, the heart is not visceral. It is sentimental, and in it is born the decision to seek and find Him.

2) Verse 9: "Jehovah will receive us, let us cry out to Him (prayer and worship)." The face, more than an aesthetic image, is the personality, the reflection of intentions, and the expression of human emotions. But in the case of God, it means mercy, goodness, and love. God's face is the entrance to heaven, and when He bows to us, blessings of help and protection are poured out. Creation, the Bible, Jesus, and the Holy Spirit are the distinguishing features that make the divine face unique.

3) Verse 10: "Jehovah will never reject us, He is refuge (salvation)." There is no life without disappointment or existence without loneliness. The uncertainty caused by abandonment, rejection, and betrayal destroys emotional stability and creates deep sadness and suffering. These feelings produce traumas and complexes that distance and separate the individual from family and social and spiritual interactions, confining him in a depressive state in which he or she renounces all hope of fulfillment and happiness. This often has serious and irreversible consequences, including, at times, death. But the Word of God assures

us that no matter how many and strong the obstacles, setbacks, and difficulties may be; however complicated and disadvantageous the situations, conditions, and expectations may be, Jehovah God will always address each of the needs we face on our pilgrimages along the paths of faith before reaching heaven.

These last four verses make up a testimonial block of what the Christian life should be:

1) Verse 11: "Teach me and guide me." Acquiring knowledge is a natural process of life but learning led by a teacher is for a limited time yet lasts forever. Life teaches us to survive; God teaches us to live. Existence without divine wisdom loses all its value. It becomes something tasteless that produces no pleasure or satisfaction. But when the guide of our steps is the way marked by the Word of God, nothing can stop us because the true man of faith has no enemies, only opponents of God's work. God's guidance does not mean ease or comfort but stability and constancy. God leads us on level, uniform paths, but we must walk those paths to reach our spiritual refuges. We must not

only see human beings as slaves to evil, but we must also know to detect and avoid the provocateur of evil.

2) Verse 12: "Let us seek the protection of the Father." Of all animals, the human being is the most helpless at birth and the most dependent while growing up. Therefore, they need heavenly protection from the very moment of their births, and God is the only one who can provide us with a place where we find security and salvation from the falsehoods and slanders that constantly accuse us.

3) Verse 13: "Let us trust in the Faithfulness of the Father." This verse is in tune with the popular saying, "The last thing that is lost is faith." If we have faith, we will remain standing in struggle. God's goodness is not a goal to achieve; it is a trajectory in which we enjoy God's mercy and wonders while we are going through it.

4) Verse 14: "Let us wait for the father's time." The breath of the heart is in the effort; the more we work, the better results we will have. Those who wait on Jehovah will have the strength and courage to conquer the positions given by God. From Jehovah, we must expect the fulfillment of His promises of supply, wisdom,

and protection, understanding that many times the fulfillment of these promises has no definite date. And moreover, the greatest of promises, eternal life, is to attain it in this life but to enjoy it in the afterlife.

PSALM 30

Glory, conceived as a spiritual attribute, belongs only to God. We can do nothing about it; we can only worship it. Jehovah is glorious because of His holiness, majesty, and authority. Everything we see God doing is due to His glory, from which emanates the power to make His decisions. Jehovah saves us because in His eyes, we are highly esteemed, which makes us feel exalted, and being deserving of God's attention is the greatest privilege bestowed on a human being. Glorifying God demands total surrender in body, soul, and spirit, all surrendered to Him in absolute prostration of attitudes and capacities. The manifestation of the magnificent divine glory sets back the strategies of destruction that may be raised against the children of God. In Jehovah's glory shines His beauty. His goodness is poured out, and there lies the grace that spreads over the whole earth.

There are three health systems:

1) The natural: immune system
2) The human: medicine
3) The divine: the action of God's power

Apparently in this case, the disease had defeated the immune system and the medicine, making it necessary to resort to the power of God, who overcomes everything to perform a miracle. Crying is the master key that opens the chest of blessings. Divine goodness has sensitive ears to human pain and tragedies. God is for us, He loves us, and His healing is our relief and comfort. By the wounds made on the body of Jesus, we are healed. Let us bring our sick and suffering life before the heavenly doctor, and we will find the necessary comfort because God's sweet and tender hand as it glides delicately upon us is a balm that relieves and eliminates the pain that oppresses and saddens us. Really, the biggest disease is being away from Him.

All diseases are not the same. Some kill the body; others kill the spirit. Those that kill the body are temporary, but those that kill the spirit are eternal. Although we are completely healthy physically, many times we feel that spiritually, we are on the edge of the abyss and have desires to let ourselves fall into the void. It often happens that the road seems to end, and the space to advance is finished. But it also seems that there is no propitious place for us on earth, and so we renounce to heal the sores that burn the skin. We accept as personal fatalism that suffering is the payment of our faults, forgetting that we have a benevolent redeemer, who lifts us up from the discouragement that overwhelms us by imposing hope on adversity to vivify the fainting spirit with new energy, new opportunities, and new beginnings. God does not want to see us go down to the grave but to go up to heaven. So, He gives us life in His only begotten Son, Jesus Christ.

Healing, life, and salvation are sung. The song commemorates, exalts, praises, and demonstrates the feelings we celebrate for the favors received. Gratitude creates songs in the soul that overflow to the only One who deserves it, Jehovah. He is holy, and only the music of the saints pleases His ears. Holiness only accepts holiness.

Jehovah's wrath is a derivation of His love for humankind, so it does not endure or harm. Instead, it instructs and edifies to forgive and restore. God's anger means that something is separating us from Him, which diminishes His influence in our lives, preventing the flow and presence of the Holy Spirit who restores, guides, and blesses us. The spiritual night may seem long to us, but it will always be temporary. There will be a tomorrow that will bring a new, radiant dawn of light that defeats darkness. But the nights can be helpful if we harness them for the benefit of the kingdom in prayer, meditation, and faith-building. During the nights, the power of God also works and is manifested. Therefore, in them we must also rejoice, despite the darkness. In the darkness of their night of captivity, beaten and chained, Paul and Silas sang songs of praise. Then God shook the prison, opened the doors, and released the chains that bound them. Let us praise God in the darkness of the nights until the morning comes, full of joy and joy for the wonders that will be done in our lives.

In confidence is the danger. Once protected, saved, and affirmed in the victory that divine benevolence has bestowed on us, it is easy to believe that favor is permanent, and we are invaded by an attitude of security that can become arrogance. We are children of God, but this does not make us better. It makes us different. Believers in Christ possess a spiritual force coming from the Holy Spirit that adds supernatural energy to natural life, providing the necessary spiritual endurance that overcomes the world. We must not allow this to become vanity. Our achievements are not decorations but gifts.

In 1 Corinthians 10:12, the Bible says, "Wherefore let him that thinketh he standeth take heed lest he fall." Stability does not depend on body balance; it depends on attitude. Staying is not a fortuitous act of balance; it is a decision carefully analyzed and firmly made. Every step forward is a risk of regression. Every step climbed presents a danger of falling. Occupying a spiritual position with authority and capacity to defy the contrary onslaughts during the journey of faith requires taking precautions that avoid being surprised. Having specific plans, tactics, and strategies ensure that you retain the spiritual location that pleases God. Under no circumstances, does confidence in us guarantee God's favor. Only the attitude of dependence on Him will make it possible to preserve the blessings obtained.

The life of faith is a cry of supplication to Jehovah and the Lord, who are Jehovah the Lord and God the Father, God the Son, and God the Holy Spirit. The divine Trinity was openly manifested in the New Testament, but it already existed and manifested itself before and throughout the Old Testament.

Making mistakes is different from sinning. Anyone can be wrong because of ignorance, recklessness, or impatience. But to sin is knowing the Word, will, and teaching of God yet going against them voluntarily and deliberately. Apparently, this is the case exposed in verses 6 and 7. David felt so confident and sure of himself that he forgot to give honor and glory to the sovereign of Israel. Verse 8 is the attempt to make amends for that sin. Everything we have comes from God, and we must give grace for it. Forgetting about worship and devotion is a frequent reason God hides His face from us.

Trying to persuade God with excuses is not a plausible method of obtaining forgiveness. He searches hearts, knows plans, and discovers intentions. What advantage is there in dying? A lot: "We are confident, I say, and willing rather to be absent from the body, and to be present with the Lord" (2 Corinthians 5:8). Shall the dust praise you? "And he answered and said unto them, I tell you that, if these should hold their peace, the stones would immediately cry out" (Luke 19:40). Will announce your truth? Of course. That's why Jesus came, "to preach the acceptable year of the Lord" (Luke 4:19). Nothing will prevent the gospel of Jesus Christ from being proclaimed throughout the earth. "And this gospel of the kingdom shall be preached in all the world for a witness unto all nations; and then shall the end come" (Matthew 24:14). The goal of the Great Commission is not to fill the church but to provoke the second coming of Jesus Christ to seek his bride dressed in fine linen to celebrate the marriage of the lamb in heaven.

The only way to ask God for forgiveness is to come into His presence, repent of one's sins, and be determined not to commit them again because it damages the relationship with Him. We must acknowledge our faults and understand that they cannot be forgiven based on our goodness but only by His grace and mercy. He is the only One who has provided the means, methods, and the result to be accepted again into His presence as beloved children. Jesus alone has the power and authority to help us with salvation.

The passing of time does not make things better; it makes them worse. Time makes things older, worn out, and destroyed. It is a lie that brings oblivion and feelings of being defeated. The weariness of living distresses and extenuates. Walking is painful, and the only way out seems to be to give up. Time becomes the punishment of life without hope. How can we make it useful?

Give it to God. He turns it into moments of encounter, change, and beginning. He is eternal and has no need to measure the course of His existence. It has been us, with our limitations, who have established a system of measures to mark points of reference in human history. In God's infinite time, life develops. We are temporary passengers of His eternity. The past is diluted by divine will and turned into the beginning of a different future. Although we are enduring the greatest of abandonments and going through the cruelest of sufferings, in the next instant, it can be transformed into joy and dance by and for the heavenly Lord, who holds souls in the palm of his hand.

Sackcloth, in ancient times, was a rough garment made of animal hair deliberately used to cause discomfort and itching in its wearing. It was used to show penance, grief, and repentance for something or someone. The sackcloth of spiritual life is everything that affects our relationships with God and separates us from Him. Without realizing it and assuming we are obeying, we still make many mistakes because we obey in our own ways, not as God specifically ordained in His sacred Word. An example of this is Abram, who obeyed in his own way when God said to him, "Now the Lord had said unto Abram, get thee out of thy country, and from thy kindred, and from thy father's house, unto a land that I will shew thee" (Genesis 12:1). But Abram undertook the journey (obedience) with his nephew Lot (his kindred, disobedience), which caused him trouble and setbacks when they arrived in the Promised Land. This is also true in our cases. We pretend to obey by following our rules, and we will never please God by acting in this way. Obedience must be exactly as stated in the Bible. Our sackcloth garments will be untied when our behaviors do not denigrate obedience due to divine orders, and we are invested with the joy that emanates from God's heart.

The blessings of protection, liberation, and emancipation from oppressions sometimes fall prey to attacks and threats that endanger personal, emotional, and spiritual stability. When they occur in life, there is endless music in the soul that reaches the throne of grace, where Jesus sits at the right hand of the Father. There he intercedes for us so that there is no lack of guidance, revelation, and power of the Holy Spirit in our lives. Our lives are illuminated in the way of redemption through faith in our Lord and Savior, Jesus Christ, the only begotten Son of God, the One who lived and died for the forgiveness of sins and rose again to give us eternal life together with Him in the presence of the Father.

PSALM 32

We are born and live exposed to sin. Transgressions happen because we seek and commit them. The tendency to separate ourselves from God is innate. It is wrong to blame circumstances, needs, or society for our sins and disobediences since we have God's infallible guidance in His written Word to conduct ourselves properly according to His will and to please Him. Responsibility for our actions is always personal; that is why salvation is individual. God's grace, defined as undeserved divine favor, covers our outbursts, our involuntary thoughts, and all that is born in the flesh but does not become sin. Ephesians 4:26 defines it thus: "Be ye angry, and sin not; let not the sun go down upon your wrath." We must know how to control the carnal impulses caused by circumstantial stimuli to avoid transgressing the law of God and not cause damage to the image of Christ before humankind.

A blessed person is one who enjoys that unmerited favor of God (grace) and is therefore happy and prosperous. That favor forgives sins and covers transgressions, which provides us with spiritual peace because Jehovah does not blame us for our iniquities or find deceptions in us. The blessed one walks on a firm foot, smiles broadly, and lives to the fullest. A blessing, although it has an influence on the material, is primarily trusting that God's assurance assists us in a special way during difficulties and leads us to the Lord's peace and freedom. The blessed count on God (Matthew 5:3–12).

Forgiveness is not automatic. There is an indispensable requirement to obtain it. You must ask for it. Hidden, unconfessed sin is fire that burns the soul and extinguishes the spirit, turning us away from God. The more we retain sin, the greater the internal damage it causes, and the greater the distance it establishes between guilt and justification. Although God knows everything, He requires a declaration of sin to grant a condemnation annulment agreement. Confession is equivalent to liberation. Having knowledge of what separates us from God and not solving it affects the human environment and context in which we live. Let us talk to God to silence the weeping that consumes our souls.

The first direct consequences of keeping our sins unconfessed are separation, absence, and loss of God's presence, blessing, and protection. One of the underlying ideas behind the concept of sin is to miss the target, which in the spiritual realm refers to leading our lives toward wrong behaviors. Because sin is rebellion, the negative results of our actions do not take long to appear, and projects, plans, and dreams do not materialize as planned or are not realized. It's not God's fault. It's our fault.

God intends for our circumstances to be comfortable and propitious. It is we who make them difficult. But at the same time, Jehovah turns these situations into reasons to approach Him and produce the brokenness that leads us to the confession of guilt and request forgiveness. And once granted, His forgiveness moves us to the position of innocence. We are exonerated from the sentence we must pay because we are attributed the payment Jesus made on the cross for the guilt of believers.

Prayer is God's established method for the saints to communicate with Him. Prayer introduces us to the spiritual environment within the divine reality. Through prayer, the grammatical meanings of the words are transformed into kindred impulses with the Holy Spirit flow. The feelings and needs that overwhelm us are transferred to God. The saints are not the ones on the altars to be worshipped but those who have given their lives to Jesus. The quality of saint is not a postmortem title. It is an attitude to life, a way of living to please God. Finding Jehovah is only possible before He returns or before we die. Since either possibility can happen suddenly, we should not postpone receiving Jesus as our Lord and Savior. The next second may be late.

Carefully analyzing these two possibilities—rapture or death—we realize that we are one instant away from eternity. There may not be a next heartbeat, or maybe in the next second, rapture will happen. Let us become aware of the urgent need to give our lives to Jesus Christ, who was sent to save the world and is the only one with the power, authority, and will free us from the flood of contradictions that overwhelm us. When the strongest helps us, there is nothing to fear.

The true refuge that the soul needs is found only in communion with the Holy Spirit, seeking His presence, and following His instructions. Shelters must be impregnable, offering the total security of salvation to those who shelter in it. Jehovah alone meets these requirements: "The Lord is good, a strong hold in the day of trouble" (Nahum 1:7), "The name of the Lord is strong tower" (Proverbs 18:10), "and that he is a rewarder of them that diligently seek him" (Hebrews 11:6). By confessing our sins, the anguish disappears, and leaving room for rejoicing at being restored in the spiritual relationship that belongs to us by nature. To be free is not to do what we want, but to be where we should. Freedom is flowing in God's will and being a channel of blessing.

To understand, you must be taught; and to teach, you must have understood. One of the immanent characteristics of the deity is omniscience, which means that God knows everything. Therefore, He has full understanding of cosmic, earthly, and human processes, possessing the maximum wisdom existing in the universe. This category of omniscient qualifies Him as the best qualified teacher to make us understand our reasons for being and showing us His ways and purposes with the aim of achieving the full realization of the human being through the recovery of His original holy spiritual essence, with which we were created. All the truths necessary to be saved have been revealed to us in the gospel of Jesus Christ.

The difference that separates animals from humans is reasoning. Animals are instinctive, and we are rational. They must be led with reins, and we are guided by instructions. The animal kingdom has no awareness of a higher being who rules destinies. Human beings possess spirituality that reveals the presence of something above the known that governs the relationships and development of the universe. We are honored to know that there is a true, creative, and powerful God. And as believers, we have the privilege of living in communion with Him through faith in the eternal and sufficient sacrifice that His Son, Jesus, made on the cross on Calvary.

Impiety is painful because of the events and circumstances that produce it and the consequences resulting from it. There is no gain in being ungodly. The most consistent way to achieve a solid, stable, and fulfilling life is to follow the Christian moral principles set forth in the Gospels. Waiting on Jehovah is not leisure. It is hard work in establishing the kingdom of God on earth. The attitude of waiting requires patience as the fruit of the Spirit surrounds us with heavenly blessings on earth.

Printed in the United States
by Baker & Taylor Publisher Services